Dare 2 Dream Leaders Inc.

Present

Beyond Career Day

A Success Guide for Middle School Youth

Written By Ijana Nathaniel

Dear Richard

I hope this
book motivates
and inspires.

Dream Big !

Ijana

Ijana Nathaniel

Brooklyn, New York

Cover - Editing- Interior Layout: Robin E. Devonish, The Self-Publishing Maven

Formatting: Tri Admojo

ISBN-13: 978-09973841-0-9

ISBN-10: 0997384107

Ijana Nathaniel

https://about.me/ijana.nathaniel

ijananathaniel@gmail.com

347-560-9836

Social Media Platforms

@ijananathaniel

Printed in the United States of America

Acknowledgements

To every young person reading this right now, this book is dedicated to you. I wrote this book with you in mind. I believe in you, and I want you to know that you have the tools within you to succeed. All you need to do is believe in yourself, never stop learning and always pay it forward, which means to share your gifts and talents to help others. I believe this book will be a great tool to help nurture your unique skills and lead you on your road to success.

Thank you to everyone who believed in me and encouraged me to write this book and to dream big. This includes my dad, my brothers, extended family, friends, and my entire Board of Directors at Dare 2 Dream Leaders Inc. Special recognition to Francis Clifford, my friend and Board Member who has always supported me and Jamillah Williams –Tetterton, my supportive cousin for both donating towards our Beyond Career Day Periscope Fundraiser. It was individuals like them who made this book possible.

To my aunt Roxanne who named me her She-Ro for doing too much at one time. I want to thank you for being one of my biggest cheerleaders.

I want to thank anyone who had a part in making this book a reality. If you gave me advice, listened to my ideas, provided training and coaching to me during this process or was just a good friend to me. Thank you for being there, I truly appreciate you all.

Last but not least, I want to dedicate this book to my children Jeremiah and Nia Renee. You are the reason I live and strive to be great. I want you to see that you can do anything you put your mind to. You inspire me to be a better person and mother. You teach me how to love. For this, I thank you and love you both.

Table of Contents

Introduction

What is Beyond Career Day all about? Every year schools across the country design an event for their junior high school seniors called Career Day. The purpose of this day is to prepare students for the career world and introduce them to individuals working in various fields in hopes to motivate youth to go to college and have a great career.

Beyond Career Day is a book designed to prepare you for career day and beyond. Sadly, many students your age and stage of life have no idea what career path they want to take, or they know what they want to do. However, they don't know what steps they need to take in getting there.

Reader, this book will:

1. Show you how to design the life you want in a cool and fun way.

2. Show you that there is more to life than just having a job.

3. Provide you with unique ways for you to create your own money.

4. Give you unique, simple examples on how you can start a business.

5. Prepare you for job interviews and how to professional dress for success.

6. Provide our top tips on how to build your resume.

7. Remind you how being a part of community service projects can help you succeed while doing good deeds for others.

8. Give you tips on how to save the money you earn, budget and invest it so it can grow.

9. Help you negotiate more money for things you may already be doing in your home.

10. Encourage you to be confident and bold.

Huge bonus! This guide has a built in Dream Board section just for you. A Dream Board is a fun way to map out the goals you want to accomplish in life. For example, if you want to attend a particular school next year, you would add the name of the school or even a photo of the school on your Dream Board, or if you want to begin working at Google after you graduate college, you would add this to your Dream Board. More about Dream Boards later in this success guide.

"Do not leave this world without giving it your all."

-Tupac Shakur

Chapter 1
Dreams + Action = Success

Hello Greatness,

I want you to know that your wildest dreams are waiting for you to wake up and turn them into a reality. Your dream board is about you. It is not about the YOU that you see now, but the YOU that is to come.

The beauty about your dream is that, it is possible. I want you to make sure that you pick a big dream to put right in the middle of your board. Next, I want you to own your dream by putting your name on the top of your dream board and even add a picture of yourself. You know that hot selfie picture on your dream board and put your name and then these words, "The Great" next to your name. (e. g. Lucinda, The Great). Now, your turn. Last, I want you to get comfy, turn on your favorite song, make yourself a cup of your favorite beverage, and let's get to work.

Dream boards don't work for everyone. This is because most people begin DREAM boarding without getting clear on what they desire in their life. Most people don't know what they want. Being clear on your desires is necessary so that your DREAM board is filled with images that connect with your purpose and not your ego. A DREAM board must be created with gratitude, appreciation, confidence, positive intention, a sense of worthiness and the freedom to flow. This means you leave the perfectionist out of the process.

Your DREAM board should not contain a shopping list or wish list of outer things. Your DREAM board should contain more of what peace, love, success and happiness looks like for you. Ask yourself what do I _____desire? Keep asking yourself this question until you release any superficial thoughts of external things that will make you happy and more of what the heart is telling you to embrace. External things are great for enjoyment, but I want you to focus on personal fulfillment of your hearts desires first.

Clear? Okay so let's move on.

The images and words you will paste on your board should serve like a GPS or Navigation system. Have an overflowing feeling and belief that you can truly have whatever you put on your board and in fact you already have it. Before any images are selected and glued it is important to have cleared out any limiting beliefs that may stop you from believing you have the power to enjoy the presence of your desired experience, person, place or thing in your life. If you don't believe that you are entitled to or can bring about the things you placed on your board, then you will block them from coming to you. It's all about faith. Release any negative thoughts and emotions, and create your board feeling inspired, excited and enthused. This is the secret most 5 year old children have and that adults are trying to embrace. You are somewhere in the middle, so you can do it. "You can be, do and have all that your hearts desires, even a pink unicorn with purple polka dots.

Positioning:

Once completed it is crucial to hang your board somewhere that you actively spend the majority of your day. Poor positioning is something can completely stifle DREAM board success. Many people create beautiful boards filled with inspiring images that celebrate their greatest DREAM for themselves, then hide the board in a cupboard or hang it up in a room they never use. Place your board eye level in a space where it can be admired and appreciated regularly. The best place to hang your board is in your office or living room. The more time you spend with your board, the more movement, you will make toward your goals and the faster they will manifest into reality. What you think about you become.

Give yourself permission to explore the things that you really desire to welcome more of in your life.

Ask yourself the following questions:

What would I like to be, do or have in my life if I knew it was okay to have anything I desired?

If I knew, I deserved it?

If I knew, I could succeed?

If I had no fear or doubt?

If I had abundant resources and all the time I needed?

Bold Statement:

If you are not clear on your mission in life, it's not too early to see and find it. Take three deep breaths, turn your focus inward and ask yourself "what am I here to do." Notice what thoughts, feelings or sensations you get. Write your bold statement in the first person, e.g. "I am a positive leader, making a positive difference in the lives of at risk youth." Underneath your bold statement write the things you will experience as you actualize this DREAM of yourself, e.g. "I am happy, wealthy and healthy. I have loving relationships; I experience prosperity and abundance in all areas of my life. I enjoy giving and receiving wealth and knowledge".

Write your bold statement accompanied by a current photo of yourself at the center of your board.

Have fun and enjoy. This is an ongoing process as your DREAM board begins to unfold so will your courage to dream bigger. Please make sure you tag me on social media with an image of your Masterpiece. Please keep in mind there is no right or wrong way to create a DREAM board. What's, even more, exciting is you can start right here in this chapter.

Enjoy!

Lucinda Cross, Vision Board Expert

Ask yourself right now, if I knew I couldn't fail, what would I do? Write it here:

Impossible Is Nothing – Muhammad Ali

So give it your all and be the best you that you can be!

This chapter is all about **YOU**. In the next few pages, you are going to think about all of the things you want in life. What kind of clothes do you like to wear, what type of house do you want to live in, what are your favorite foods, what type of job you want to have, and where do you want to travel, and much more.

What I want you to do next is **IMAGINE** and **DREAM BIG**!

1) What do you like to do for fun?

Do you like to play video games, ride your bike, cook, bake, talk on the phone, watch movies, travel, etc.? Write your answers below.

_____

_____

_____

_____

_____

2) What are your unique skills?

Do you like to make jewelry, build things, sing, make music, create videos, design clothing, write stories or poetry etc.? Write your answers below.

_____

_____

_____

_____

_____

3) If you could vacation anywhere, where would you go?

Imagine yourself on the best vacation ever. Is it hot? Is it cold? Are you on a Boat? Are you on the beach? Etc.? Write your answers below.

_____

_____

_____

_____

_____

4) What High School do you want to attend?

Think about your dream job/career and ask yourself, is this school going to prepare me for college? What are their graduation rates, meaning, how many students graduate on time from this high school? What does your grade point average have to be in order to apply to this school? Does this school prepare you for college? Write your answers below.

_____

_____

_____

_____

_____

5) What college do you want to attend?

Ask yourself, does this college have what I want to help me get my dream job. Think of what you want to learn, the type of activities you want to participate in. Do I want to go away to college? Do I want to live at home and go to college? Write your answers below.

_____

_____

_____

_____

_____

6) What is your dream job?

Think of your how much money you want to earn, will this job make you happy? Does your job help you to help others? Are you a chef, teacher, police officer, doctor, hair stylist, author, fashion designer or something else? Write your answers below.

_____

_____

_____

_____

_____

7) What is your ideal fitness goal?

Imagine how healthy you want to be right now and when you become an adult. What does that look like to you? There is a popular saying which states, 'Your health is your wealth'. This means that if you are not healthy, you are limited to doing all of the things in life that you dream of. So choose to be healthy. Write your answers below.

_____

_____

_____

_____

_____

8) How can you be of service?

Ask yourself what are the things you care about the most? Do you have a desire to feed the homeless, do you love animals, do you want to help the environment, and do you want to help others be healthy? Write your answers below.

_____

_____

_____

_____

_____

Have you ever wished you could create and design the life you want to live?

Now you can!

Design Your Dream Board

Step 1:

Using the answers from the 8 above questions, use pictures, quotes, and or written statements to create your dream board.

Getting started creating your dream board: Look around your house for old magazines that are not in use or your school may have some magazines that you can use as well. No need to purchase new magazines for this activity. Begin to cut our photos of the things that you want in life.

Tools needed: Scissors, Glue, Magazines. Use the bank pages in the next section for your dream board. *(Feel free to add color, glitter, stickers, personal photos and family photos as well)*.

See below for a few tips on what you may want to cut out and add to your dream board.

1. If you want to live in a house, you may want to cut out a photo of your dream house.

2. Did you say you want a nice car? You can find picture of a car to add to your board.

3. You can find a photo of a school or college to represent you wanting to go to school.

4. Are you dreaming of going on vacation? You can find a picture of the place you want to visit.

5. Do you love to shop or like to dress nice? You can add the latest fashions to your dream board.

6. Need a little inspiration? Cut our words that motivate you. You can even find quotes to cut out and add to your board.

7. Once you have all of the pictures cut out, arrange them on the board to see how you would like them to be displayed.

8. Once you have the photos laid out like you like it, glue them down and wait for it all to dry. Ta Da! You have your very own DREAM BOARD!

Step 2: Set S.M.A.R.T Goals.

S= Specific M= Measurable A= Attainable R= Realistic T=Timely. Be specific about our goals. Say what you mean, mean what you say and measure the time and energy it is going to take to reach them. Set start and end dates for your goals. Doing this allows you to always focus on your dreams and what you want to accomplish. Set attainable goals, which means, goals that you know you can actually accomplish. For example, I plan to get all A's in the spring semester. I plan to get my driver's license by the time I am 16 years old or within two years. Keep it real with yourself and set realistic goals. Last, be timely and do not set goals so far out that you will forget about them.

Step 3: Take action or like NIKE says JUST DO IT!

For example, if your dream is to learn how to dance, you can sign up for a dance class or log into YouTube and search for the dance you want to learn for FREE.

Dreams + Action = Success
Begin Dreaming

Add photo's, quotes, words describing question's 1-8

Dream Big   IMAGINE   B   Dare 2 Be   ANYTHING IS POSSIBLE
                        e   Different
         Be Creative   y
                        o
                        u

Dream Big   Be Creative   IMAGINE   Be you   Dare 2 Be Different   ANYTHING IS POSSIBLE

Dream Big
Be Creative
IMAGINE
Be You
Dare 2 Be Different
ANYTHING IS POSSIBLE

Dream Big   Be Creative   IMAGINE   Be You   Dare 2 Be Different   ANYTHING IS POSSIBLE

"Dreams do come true if you believe in yourself. Anything is possible."

– Jennifer Capriati

Chapter 2
Who Am I

If someone asked you to describe yourself, what would you say? Now that you have created your dream board, and have identified your short term and long term goals, you're ready for the next step; an activity called "Who Am I." Write down 8 words that can describe who you are. Not what you do, but who you are.

I AM Examples: I am a good listener, I am a loving person, and I'm a giver. **Remember** who you are, is what makes you unique. Do not strive to be anyone but the best YOU that you can be.

1) _____

2) _____

3) _____

4) _____

5) _____

6) _____

7) _____

8) _____

The next step of the WHO AM I activity is to learn about a bit more about yourself. In this activity write down things you do well, things you struggle with, what resources you have around you to help you succeed including money, friends, family, teachers, etc. Last, what are your fears? What can get in the way of you being a success?

Once you know this, you will know what you're good at, what you need to seek help with, who you have for support and help. Also, you will know what your fears are so you can confront them and move on towards success! Write in each section below.

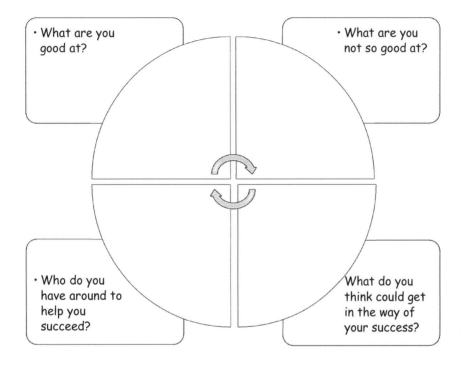

- What are you good at?

- What are you not so good at?

- Who do you have around to help you succeed?

What do you think could get in the way of your success?

"Watch your thoughts, they become words;

watch your words, they become actions;

watch your actions, they become habits;

watch your habits, they become character;

watch your character, for it becomes your destiny."

- Frank Outlaw

The above quote is so true. I want to challenge you to write a letter to your future self. In the letter, tell yourself what you want to be doing in life by the time you are 25. Give your older self-advice on life and tips on how to stay on track and not to mess up the future you. How will you tell them to conquer their fears and live their dreams?

Today's Date: _____/_____/_____

Dear future self,

_____

_____

_____

_____

_____

_____

_____

_____

_____

_____

_____

_____

_____

_____

_____

_____

_____

_____

SUCCESS

Try Harder

Fail

D2DL's

8 steps to success

Dream

Try

Think

Action

Plan

1) **Dream** – I know everyone says this, but it is true. You can do anything you put your mind to, so dream big! If you want to own your very own Cup Cake Restaurant or become the greatest Neuro Surgent, just know exactly what it takes to get there.

2) **Think** – Think before you act.

3) **Plan** – You must be ready for the opportunity. Having a plan is the key.

4) **Action** – You have your dream, you have your plan, now get to working it!

5) **Try** – Learn something new every day of your life.

6) **Fail** – Don't look at failure as a negative. Look at it as you tried something and learn from it. Turn your failure into opportunity.

7) **Try Harder** – Your failure should make you try harder because you can now use what you learned to do better the next time.

8) **Success** – Follow these steps and you will be successful.

"The way to get started is to stop talking and begin doing."

\- Walt Disney

Chapter 3
Prep for Success!

In this chapter, you will discover what the words 'Career Etiquette' mean. When you hear the word etiquette, many of you may think of learning how to use the proper fork during dinner or at a restaurant. Career etiquette is learning the proper way to prepare for an interview and how to make yourself attractive to the company seeking to hire you. In this chapter, you will learn interviewing skills, how to create a resume, how to search for a job and/or volunteer position, the importance of body language and how to dress for success. As a **Bonus**, chapter 7 will provide sample resumes, cover letters and pictures showcasing different categories of professional wear.

8 STEPS TO WRTITNG A WINNING RESUME

1) **Step 1:** Include your full name, address, **PROFESSIONAL** email address and telephone number at the top of your resume.

2) **Step 2:** Create a story about yourself in the form of a short **summary** (see sample resume for examples). The summary will include things you do well, something you are an expert in and who you are as a person. Review your answers from the "Who AM I" chapter.

3) **Step 3:** Add your job experience. Of course, we know that at this age you may have little to no work experience for the job that you are looking to apply for. Therefore, add any volunteer positions you have done here. Volunteering is great because you are being of service, but it is also a great way to build your resume and make you attractive to the company you are interviewing with (this will be discussed further in chapter 6). Dare 2 Dream Leaders Inc. is an organization that allows youth to participate in volunteer activities throughout the year. Find an organization that you can participate in volunteer projects.

4) **Step 4 Bonus Tip:** If you are advanced and have actual work experience, you want to add that information under job experience. Examples of

jobs that you may have had, but did not consider them to be jobs include, babysitting, animal sitting, dog walking, selling candy, lemonade stand, etc. If you do not have this experience, that is ok. Work on participating in volunteering activities.

5) **Step 5:** Add the education section. This should include the full name of your school, including your grade and your GPA (Grade Point Average) and years attended (i.e. September 2012-2015). In this section, you can get creative by adding classes that you have high grades in. For example, if you have a grade of 90% - 100% you want to highlight this in your resume (see sample resume),

6) **Step 6:** Are you a member of any organization such as the Girl Scouts, Church group? You can add this to your resume as well in the section called Affiliations. This shows that you not only go to school, volunteer, work but also invest time in yourself.

7) **Step 7 Bonus Tip:** Have you received a certificate for doing excellent work? You want to share this on your resume. This also can confirm what you added as your strengths in the beginning of your resume in the summary section. Have you ever received any awards? Student of the month, Girls Scout/Boy Scout badges, leadership awards, etc. This is another great way to make you stand out from all of the other resumes. Again if you do not have everything in these 8 steps, that is fine. Highlight the best of all you have.

8) **Step 8:** Make sure you have three people, other than family, that can provide a letter of recommendation and reference for you. Employers want to hear what other people have to say about you. They want to know that they are making a good decision to hire you. Therefore, be sure to form a professional relationship with teachers, parents of friends, employees, and others who have the ability to write these letters for you.

"Build – A – Resume"

Read the scenario below and create a resume based on the details provided about Nia Campbell and do your best to create a resume for Nia.

Nia Campbell attends James Madison High School and is in her senior year. She lives at 123 ABC Lane, Brooklyn, NY 11111. Her email is NiaCampbell@abc.com, and her phone number is (555) 555-7777. Nia is very popular in school because she participates in various clubs. She is a team captain on the volleyball team as well as the editor of the school newspaper club. After school, she is the neighborhood dog walker and walks about 4 dogs per day. She has been a dog walker since October 2013.

Nia has been on the honor roll each year since her sophomore year in High School. When she was in the 10th grade, she took on a babysitting job taking care of her neighbor's 8-year-old daughter. The babysitting job lasted for one year from September 2012 to October 2013. She is always on time for school and work. She is respectful and top of her class. Nia wants to become a veterinarian because she loves animals.

(First & Last Name) _____

(Address) _____

(Telephone Number) _____

(Email) _____

Summary of qualifications:

Volunteer Experience

Volunteer position #1

Name of company:
Job Title:
Month/Year Attended:
Description of job duties:

Volunteer Experience

Volunteer position #2

Name of company:
Job Title:
Month/Year Attended:
Description of job duties:

Job Experience

Job #1

Name of company:
Job Title:
Month/Year Attended:
Description of job duties:

Job Experience

Job #2

Name of company:
Job Title:
Month/Year Attended:
Description of job duties:

Education

Name of School:
Years Attended:
GPA:
Classes w/grade of 90% and above:

Affiliations

Organizations you are a member of and your title:
Ex. Girl Scout, Brownie

Certificates

Name of Certificate and year given. Example: Math Excellence Certificate, 2012

Awards

Name of Award and year given. Example: Honor Roll Award, 2012

References furnished upon request

Your Dream Job/Volunteer Position has a position available.
Design the resume that will make them choose YOU!

(First & Last Name) _____

(Address) _____

(Telephone Number) _____

(Email) _____

Summary of qualifications:

Volunteer Experience

Volunteer position #1

Name of company:
Job Title:
Month/Year Attended:
Description of job duties:

Volunteer Experience

Volunteer position #2

Name of company:
Job Title:
Month/Year Attended:
Description of job duties:

Job Experience

Job #1

Name of company:
Job Title:
Month/Year Attended:
Description of job duties:

Job Experience

Job #2

| Name of company: |
| Job Title: |
| Month/Year Attended: |
| Description of job duties: |
| |
| |
| |
| |
| |
| |

Education

| Name of School: |
| Years Attended: |
| GPA: |
| Classes w/grade of 90% and above: |
| |
| |
| |

Affiliations

| Organizations you are a member of and your title: |
| Ex. Girl Scout, Brownie |
| |
| |
| |
| |

Certificates

Name of Certificate and year given. Example: Math Excellence Certificate, 2012

Awards

Name of Award and year given. Example: Honor Roll Award, 2012

References furnished upon request

TOP 8 <u>BEFORE</u> & <u>AFTER</u> INTERVIEWING TIPS

1) **Do your research** – Google.com is your friend. Research the organization for which you are seeking to be hired. Know their mission, vision statement and what they do. Huge! Find out who is interviewing you.

2) **Practice! Practice! Practice!** – Review the list of interviewing questions shared in this success guide. Practice your response before the interview. Practice having eye contact with your interviewer and giving firm handshakes. Eye contact lets your interviewer know that you are interested and giving a firm handshake shows you are confident.

3) **Be on time** – Always arrive at least 15 minutes early to your interview. Being late could give you a negative start, and it could prevent you from getting the position. Remember this saying "if you are early, you are on-time and if you are on-time, you are late" – Dr. Lee in Movie Drum Line

4) **Travel Alone** – This suggestion doesn't mean that you can't have an adult or someone that you trust to escort you to the interview. What this means is to travel to your interview alone, without friends. You want to remain professional at all times. With unnecessary company, you may forget that you are on an interview as you wait to be called and begin to do things that are unacceptable to the eye of the company you want to work for. For instance, with your friends you may tell jokes, giggle and laugh a lot. Remember, someone is always watching you and judging you. So be ready and prepared at all times. Remember, there is a time and place for everything.

5) **Bring your resume** – Always carry two extra resumes with you, one for the person interviewing you and the second for you to review in case you need to look at it to answer a question. Or in case, there is more than one interviewer.

6) **Be confident and smile** – Go to the interview giving it your all. You read the eight tips, and now you're ready. Even if you are nervous, smile and give a firm handshake to the interviewer.

7) **Dress for success** - Review the section "Dress 4 Success" in this book and choose an outfit similar to the category. Remember, you can never make a second 1st impression, so make the first your best.

8) **Send thank you letters** – After your interview, ask the person who is interviewing you for their information including their address, e-mail, and telephone number. Take that information and send them an e-mail thanking them for to the interview you. To make yourself stand out from the rest, mail a handwritten thank you card. Email is fine, but you always want to go above, beyond and add a more personal touch. Lastly, use the phone number to follow up with them within 2 weeks if you have not heard anything from them. It is not pushy to ask about where you are in the interview process. Remember, in the words of mogul Jay-Z, a closed mouth won't get fed.

Bonus Tip: Remember you only have one chance to make a good first impression. Therefore, put your best with everyone you meet that day. You never know who is watching you. For example, if you arrive at the interview, and they have you waiting longer than expected, be calm and patient. When your interview arrives, show that you were not bothered by the wait time, and say thank you for taking the time to meet with me. Employers love to know that their employees can adapt to change.

TOP 8 INTERVIEWING QUESTIONS & SAMPLE ANSWERS

1) **Tell me about yourself.**

   a) Answer: I am dependable, honest, reliable.

2) **Why did you apply for this position?**

   a) Answer: I am passionate about the mission of the organization, and I believe I can contribute to the success of this company with my skill set.

3) **What are your strengths?**

   a) Answer: I communicate well with others, I am a team player, and I am willing to the work get the job done.

4) **Tell us how you would handle a difficult customer.**

   a) Answer: I would listen to the customer and do my best to solve their problem. If I am unable to calm them down and help them, I would call for supervision assistance.

5) **Tell us about a challenge you faced and how you overcame it.**

   a) Answer: In class I received a low grade and in order to bring my grade back up I asked the teacher for extra work, and I also studied more.

6) **Who is the most influential person in your life and why?**

   a) Answer: The most influential person to me is my teacher because she believes in my and is always pushing me to do my best.

7) **How would you handle working with someone you do not particularly like?**

   a) Answer: I am a team player and can get along with anyone. Therefore, I do not see that being an issue.

8) Why should we hire you?

    a) You should hire me because I am a dedicated candidate with a positive attitude. I will work hard to get the job done.

PRACTICE! PRACTICE! PRACTICE! IT'S YOUR TURN. WRITE YOUR ANSWERS

1) Tell me about yourself.

```
┌──────────────────────────────────────────────┐
│                                                │
│                                                │
│                                                │
│                                                │
│                                                │
│                                                │
│                                                │
│                                                │
└──────────────────────────────────────────────┘
```

2) Why did you apply for this position?

```
┌──────────────────────────────────────────────┐
│                                                │
│                                                │
│                                                │
│                                                │
│                                                │
│                                                │
│                                                │
└──────────────────────────────────────────────┘
```

3) What are your strengths?

4) Tell us how you would handle a difficult customer.

5) Tell us about a challenge you faced and how you overcame it.

6) Who is the most influential person in your life and why?

7) How would you handle working with someone you do not particularly like?

8) Why should we hire you?

CAREER ETIQUETTE WHAT SHOULD YOU DO ACTIVITY

1 - What SHOULD you do if...

What should you do if you get a call to come in for an interview?

A. Research the company by going to their website.

B. Review the interview questions in this manual to prepare for the interview.

C. Update and review resume, and print out two resume's for the interview.

D. All of the above.

If you answered

A. Research the company by going to their website. **Correct! As stated in the previous tips, do your research.**

B. Review the interview questions in this manual to prepare for the interview. **Yes!**

C. Update and review resume, and print out two resume's for the interview. **Yes! Always be prepared.**

D. All of the above. – **If you answered D, you are absolutely CORRECT!**

2 - What SHOULD you do if...

You get a call from a job that you applied for. The company is a retail company, and their company is known worldwide. You are not sure of the pay rate for the position. What should you do?

A. Wait until the end of the interview and ask the person interviewing you what is the base pay rate for this position.

B. Google the company and search for open positions to see if they post the salary in the job description.

C. Accept the position without knowing the salary and be happy you have a job!

D. A, B, and C.

If you answered

A. Google the company and search for open positions to see if they post the salary in the job description. **Yes! You are right! Do your research. Do not make the mistake of asking a question that is given to you either through the job ad or on their website. It shows a lack of interest.**

B. Wait until the end of the interview and ask the person interviewing you what is the base pay rate for this position. **You are correct. After an interview, you are typically allowed to ask questions. If after you do your research on the company's website, and you do not see the pay rate posted, you should ask.**

C. Accept the position without knowing the salary and be happy you have a job! **Absolutely NOT! Never accept a position before you know how much they are going to pay you.** *"A closed mouth won't get fed"* -Jay-Z. So if you do not know then **ASK!**

D. A & B - **If you answered <u>D</u> you are correct answer is A and B for the very reasons stated above.**

"Dress for the job you want, not the
job you already have."

-Unknown

TO WEAR OR NOT TO WEAR

Did you know there is more than one category for dressing for success? The next few pages will describe dressing for different levels of success.

There are two types of attire when dressing for success. This depends on the type of job you are interviewing for.

What does it mean to dress professionally?

Dressing neatly?

Wearing clean clothes?

Wearing the most expensive outfit?

Not really.

1 Professional Dress

Dressing professional is different from company to company. However, there are some basic rules when dressing "professional" that can be applied to any job interview.

- Full 2 piece suit

- Solid color shirt or Blouse

- Cardigan Sweater or Blazer Jacket

- Tie, Bow Tie or Scarf

- Solid color pants (Absolutely no jeans for corporate positions)

- Dress or skirt below the knee

- Shoes or boots (No sneakers, sandals or flip-flops)

- Hair neat

- Light perfume/cologne or scented lotion

<table>
<tr><td>

Sample Professional Interview Dress Code for Females

- Pencil Skirt below the knee.
- White button up shirt or blouse (tucked in)
- Blazer /Cardigan
- Closed toe shoes (Heal 2-3 inches or less)
- Make up: light and natural colors. Unless you are interviewing for a makeup artist position. In that case, be creative.

Bonus Tip

If you carry a bag, be sure to clean it out so when you take out your note pad or resume, junk and other things don't fall out.

</td><td>

Sample Professional Interview Dress Code for Males

- Full 2 piece suite or Long pants (No jeans)
- Belt
- Button up shirt long sleeve or short sleeve.
- Tie or Bow Tie
- Blazer or sweater vest
- Shoes or Dressy Boots (No sneakers)
- Hair cut neat/braids freshly done/dreads/locs freshly twisted and pulled back if possible.

Bonus Tip

If you wear cologne, be sure that it is not too much, spray it up in the air and walk into it.

</td></tr>
</table>

What not to wear

- Neon Colors
- Large pieces of jewelry
- Sneakers
- Jeans
- Flip Flops
- Sweat Pants
- Too much perfume or cologne
- Shoes that are too high or that you cannot walk in.

When is it best to dress business casual? By doing your research of the company, you will see their company culture and then you will know how to dress.

> **#2 Business Casual Dress Code:**
>
> Business causal is a more comfortable and flexible style of dress. Clothing choices include but are not limited to:
>
> - Casual pants and skirts, khaki pants are also acceptable.
> - Sweaters
> - Flat shoes, strapped sandals.
> - For males, no tie necessary.
> - Hair neat, style can be flexible.

Examples of companies that you would dress "Professional" for an interview:

Law office: If you received an interview to volunteer or work at a law office, you know you would dress professionally because of their culture. When you imagine a lawyer, you imagine someone in a suit, with a briefcase and shoes or high heels.

Therefore, you would try to dress as close to that description as possible.

Target Department Store: If you received a job interview from Target you would think of their brand or look them on the internet. You would find that their brand colors are khaki and red. Therefore, you could assume that you could come to the interview business casual.

Bonus Tip: If a company has brand colors that they are known for, you may want to come to the interview dressed in those brand colors.

Interview Activity

You just received an interview for the company you have wanted to work for all year. List the things you are going to do to prepare for the interview by placing words around this circle.

List the company name _____

Job Title: _____

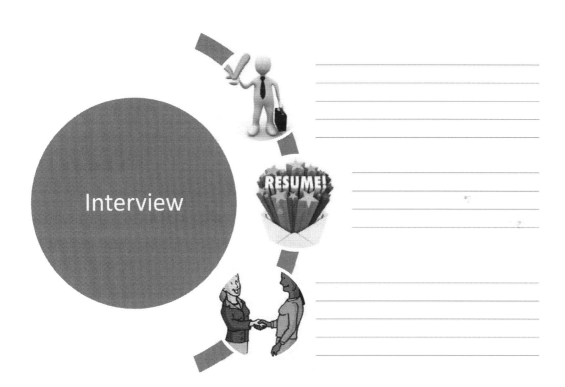

"Entrepreneurship is living a few years of your life like most people won't, so that you can spend the rest of your life like most people can't."

- Unknown

Chapter 4
There's an Entrepreneur in ALL of Us

Hey Future Superstar,

I remember being your age and sitting in a classroom just like yours, wondering what my life would be like as an adult. News flash! Don't grow up. (Bills are no fun.)

Enjoy your childhood and all that your young life has to offer. Cherish these precious moments with your friends and family. Relish in the fact that you won't be young forever but your reputation will last a life time. Your personal brand is important. What you post on social media matters. It could be the difference between you getting the job or opportunity of your dreams and not.

Hold on tight to your dreams because your dreams matter. Don't let anyone tell you that you can't make it. I am here to tell you that you can. You can be whatever your heart desires. So choose wisely and don't forget to give back to your community and the people who cared for you.

Treat your body right. Those chips and delicious chicken nuggets may come back to haunt you. Exercise daily and get lots of rest. You are going to miss those opportunities one day.

Be respectful of your parents and of your teachers. They are there to support you and see you through. If you can't find the support you need at home, look for positive role models in your community. Mentorship had opened so many doors for me and will be an integral part of your success. The adults in your life push you so hard because they believe in you. We believe in you! I need you to believe the same.

The world isn't perfect, but I know that you have what it takes to make a difference. You won't have to have all of the answers but you must be willing to give it try. You are what the world's been missing. Now is the time to dream bigger. Create a lasting ripple of impact that will benefit not just you but the people around you.

Make use of every opportunity that comes your way. Be open and willing to try something new. You never know what you are going to get. Learn a new language and travel to a foreign country. Remember, our world isn't perfect, but it's up to you to be the agent of change that you want to see. And, while you explore the world, consider being an entrepreneur. It is a viable option for a bright future. You may ask, why? Well, I have 3 reasons.

The 1st reason is entrepreneurship can be a 'Wealth Generator'. This means, if you have the desire to become wealthy, having a business is an option that can help you to reach your financial goals. The 2nd reason is entrepreneurship allows you to 'Create Your Own Opportunities'. This means, being in business gives you the flexibility to create and expand in several ways and into other business ventures. A good example of this is the rapper mogul Jay Z. He has had a record label, clothing line and presently owns a music and video website, real estate, as well as, a portion of the Brooklyn, Nets. The 3rd reason is entrepreneurship can provide you with the opporunity to 'Change and Impact the World'. Another good example of this is Oprah Winfrey who has helped many young girls in foreign countries in the area of education.

I know, the next question you have is, how do I get started? The answer is, you will learn more about it in the chapter you're about to read.

Be Amazing. Be Phenomenal. Shine Bright.

Shade Y. Adu, Teacher and Entrepreneur

There is a saying that one person should have at least seven streams of income to reach the level of financial success they want to be fiscally comfortable. What does that mean? It means that you should have seven different ways to earn money for living, saving, donating and leaving a lasting legacy.

In this chapter, you will see a formula that was created to simplify the seven and to give you a simple visual on streams of income principle. Now, just because the concept says you should have seven streams of income, it does not necessarily mean you MUST earn money all seven ways. You may be fortunate enough to only need one. However, who would turn down an opportunity to earn more money if they could? Not me? Would you? Please visit **chapter 7** for a list of resources that will guide you to developing a plan for each stream of income mentioned below.

Income Stream #1

Start a Business

I know you are saying, how do I start a business? Where do I begin? This is a question that I asked myself when I started my business. So you are not alone. I'll show you a few things that I had to do in order to figure out what I wanted to do.

Exercise #1:

Step #1: Look back at of all of the strengths you wrote down in the Who AM I during chapter 2. Write them out again.

Step# 2: Write out all of your talents and skills, if they are different from your strengths.

Step#3: Draw a $ sign next to all of the strengths, talents and skills that you know can make you money and that someone would pay you for.

Final Step: Draw a heart next to the strength, talent or skill that you would do even if no one paid you. Keep in mind, the one you pick should already have a $ sign next to it. You can love doing something, but that does not mean that it can be turned into a business.

Strengths	Talents	Skills

Income Stream #2

Write a book

Types of books you can write:

- How to: Teach someone something you know.

- Fiction: Dream up a best seller with your imagination.

- Non-Fiction: Based off of a true story. Maybe your life has some interesting inspiring or scary events that you can turn into a book.

- Visit for a complete list of other book genres http://reference. yourdictionary.com/books-literature/different-types-of-books.html

Income Stream #3

Teach

Yes, teach! That talent that you, have guess what? Not everyone knows how to do it. You can teach it one on one, in a group or worldwide by using the internet. Example: You could teach others how to do hair on YouTube, Periscope and Snap Chat or whichever video app is most popular to your audience now.

Income Stream #4

Speak

 Do you have a way with words? Do you like talking about what you are good at? Do you have an inspiring story that will help others? I think you can say yes to at least one of these. You can get paid to share information that will help others.

Income Stream #5

Invest

Do you love the latest sneakers that just came out? How about that latest piece of technology you're using? Tell your parents to buy you piece of stock from that company instead of the actual item this year for your future.

Income Stream #6

Affiliate Marketing

Did you know you could get paid from recommending someone shop at a particular store or website? Companies will pay you for telling people to shop with them at no cost to you. Example: You shop at Footlocker all the time, and people love the sneakers you wear so they ask you where they can get those same sneakers. If you are a part of Footlockers Affiliate Program, you can inform that person how to get the sneakers and give them a special code to use. Once purchased, you get paid, and it doesn't cost you a thing, accept sharing. Cool right? Now go do your research, and try it.

Income Stream #7

<u>**Create on Online Market**</u>

You can create your own products and sell them online. Example: Clothing Line, Jewelry, Customized items (redesign items you already have and make them unique and new). After you have created the list of things that you can do, pick one thing that you believe that will both earn money for you and that you love to do. Check out the resources section of this book for a link that will show you where to begin.

"Never spend your money before you have earned it.

Thomas Jefferson

Chapter 5
Young Finance
101

Dear Future Leader,

By now you've probably heard the saying "Money doesn't grow on trees." Unfortunately, it's true. But there are things you can do to ensure that you have more money in your life.

When you ask most people why they want a lot of money, most of the time it boils down to "happiness." No matter what your race, age, and religion most people just want to be happy. I'm going to tell you something that you'll hear celebrities say over and over. Money doesn't buy happiness. Yes, it buys security, but if you don't properly manage the money you have, that security can and will evaporate. Ask MC Hammer and every other celebrity or millionaire that had to declare bankruptcy. Money isn't loyal.

There are a few guiding principles when it comes to money that you should always remember no matter how little or how much you have. The first is "It is not what you earn that makes you wealthy; it is what you keep". As you grow older, you will meet people who have all of the material possessions they want. This does not make them wealthy. This makes them a hyper consumer. What makes you wealthy is having options. Not options regarding what to wear. But options regarding where to live, how long or much you have to work, how frequently you get to travel, how easily you can take care of the ones you love. The second principle to remember is: "Real wealth doesn't buy things; it buys options." You are growing up in a time where people live different lives on social media than they actually do in their real lives, celebrities included. Social media is not real life for most; it is a highlight reel.

You can't choose your family, but you can choose when you have children. You can choose who you allow into your life romantically. You can choose the friends you keep around you. Connect with people who encourage you to be better and challenge you to excel.

Traditional schooling will not teach you how to be rich, but thanks to the Internet anything you want to know is at your fingertips. Be different. Learn about things they don't teach you in school. Focus on creating freedom and options for yourself. Focus on living your life on your terms. You can now begin by reading this chapter on finances.

Be Free,

Tonya Rapley, Financial Expert

Did you know that money really does grow on trees? Just kidding! But if you manage your money the right way, you can make it grow.

After going through this chapter, you will be able to negotiate your allowance, your paycheck, and even a raise. You will also learn what it means to budget, save and invest your money. Make sure you check out the bonus tip at the end of the chapter.

What is a **budget**? Simply put, a budget is a plan for spending. It is you telling your money where to go.

There are two main categories to a budget: Income and Expenses.

Income is the money you earn every month.

Expenses are what you spend your income on every month.

Nia Renee, who is 11 years old, just got a job helping her elderly neighbor, who lives alone, walk her dog every day after school. She has agreed to pay Nia Renee $50 per week which will help Nia earn $200 per month. How cool is that? Nia also receives an allowance from her parents of $25 per month. Let's help Nia create a budget so she knows where her money will go for the month. She set a goal of only spending about 70% of her monthly earnings. Let's see if she was able to stick to her budget.

Income	Projected		Projected		Projected	
	Jan	Jan Actual	Feb	Feb Actual	Mar	Mar Actual
Job	$50	$50	$50	$50	$50	$50
Allowance	$25	$25	$25	$25	$25	$25
Total Income	$75	$75	$75	$75	$75	$75
Expenses						
Food	$15	$20	$15	$20	$15	$15
Snacks	$10	$10	$10	$15	$10	$10
Entertainment	$10	$0	$10	$20	$10	$10
Clothes	$15	$30	$15	$40	$15	$15
Total Monthly Expenses	$50	$50	$50	$95	$50	$50
Total Income	$75	$75	$75	$75	$75	$75
Remaining Balance = Income minus Expenses	$25	$25	$25	-$20	$25	$25

You just took a look at Nia's budget. Now let's explain. Nia has two forms of income. She has a dog walking job, and she receives $25 per month from her allowance. She set a monthly plan for how much she wanted to spend out of her $75 each month. These items were listed under the "Expenses" column.

There are two other words listed in the budget which are *Projected* and *Actual*.

Projected means her spending goal for the month.

Actual means what she actually spent that month.

- Did Nia Renee stick to her budget in January? Yes or No (Circle one)

- Which month did she go over her budget and why was she able to spend more than she earned for the month? _____.

  _____

  _____

- In the three months of working, how much money has Nia Renee saved?

  _____

Now it's your turn. What is your budget? Use the table below to give yourself a job or two. Create up to four monthly expenses and then create a plan for your money.

1st Calculate how much you will earn each month.

2nd Decide how much you want to spend each month over the next three months.

3rd Total up your expenses and subtract from your income to see how much you spent.

Income	Projected		Projected		Projected	
	Jan	Jan Actual	Feb	Feb Actual	Mar	Mar Actual
Job 1						
Allowance						
Total Income						
Expenses						
Total Monthly Expenses						
Total Income						
Remaining Balance = Income minus Expenses						

- How did you do? Did you go over your budget? Yes or No (Circle one)

- How much did you go over or save each month? Jan - + _____ Feb - + _____ Mar – + _____

- What were your challenges while creating a budget? _____
  _____
  _____

"You have not because you ask not."
James 4:2 -Bible

ALLOWANCE

One of the first forms of income that you may receive is from an allowance. If you do chores around the house, you are rewarded. Some parents even reward you for getting good grades. If that is you, then you are so lucky. In my house, I had to get good grades or else. Did you know that you have the power to negotiate your allowance? Just as it was said in the other quote above, you have not because you ask not.

In the Webster's Dictionary, it states the meaning of negotiation is "to discuss something formally in order to make an agreement." If you do not have an allowance, or you are trying to figure out a unique way to approach your parent or guardian for an increase in your allowance, I have a solution to your situation. Visit chapter 7 for your very own "Allowance Parent and Child Contract".

Your parent or guardian is going to either say yes or no. If they say yes, then awesome! If they say no, then use your negotiation skills and bring your fee down a bit or ask what they can afford give. If they simply say NO, that is fine as well but if you never asked you would never know. You will get many no's in life, keep trying and eventually you will get a yes. Your yes may not come from where or who you thought, but it will come eventually. Lastly, refer back to **chapter 4** and remember your skills, strengths, and talents that you could earn money from. Refer to **chapter 7** for additional entrepreneurship and job resources.

"Keep calm and save money."

- Unknown

We just went through how to create a budget. At the end of the month you want to have money left over, right? If you budget correctly, you will be able to SAVE. Savings is the money left over after you have paid everything in your budget. Savings should be SAVED, not spent right away. You should define what you are saving for.

Example: I am saving $40 for a new pair of **SHOES**. I am saving $500 for a **COMPUTER**.

Directions: In the circles below, write what the amount you want to save and you are saving for.

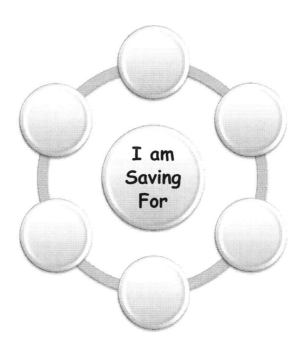

8 Saving Tips for Youth

1. Pay yourself 1st – Add yourself to your expense list to ensure that you have enough money to save.

2. Look for ways to decrease your spending in your budget and make the changes so you can save more or spend less on any item.

3. Shop Smart – There is nothing wrong with getting something on sale or using a coupon to save money.

4. Use technology to help you save and budget- See the resource section for apps you can use on your mobile phone to help you save.

5. Track your spending – Get a journal and write down everything you spend your money on and how much you spend. This will let you see where your money is going.

6. Open up a savings account!

7. Get a coin jar – Take all of your loose change and drop it into a coin jar. At the end of each month deposit it into a youth savings account.

8. Invest your savings and watch your money grow.

Which tip are you going to begin doing today? _____

_____

You now know how to budget and save. What should you do with your savings?

The answer is... **INVEST** it!

You may ask, what does it mean to invest? This term means to take your savings and place it somewhere that will help it to grow. Places to invest your money include CD's, Stocks, Bonds, Money Market Accounts and Mutual Funds. These investments grow your money over a long period of time. The length of time to invest is up to you, but money is normally put away to grow for a minimum of 3 to 5 years. To get the most out of your investment, you set up an account and leave a certain amount for over 20 years towards your retirement.

Here is an example of a way you could try to invest your savings now. Think of your favorite toy, piece of technology or favorite sneaker company. Is this company making money and showing great results? If yes, then you may want to buy a share of this company's stock or have your parent, godparent or grandparent to purchase a share of stock as a gift for you during the next holiday. If you do this, by the time you are an adult, your savings account will have grown exceedingly.

What are some of your favorite stores to shop in?

What are f your favorite sneaker brands?

What is your favorite cell phone company?

What brand computer(s) are you using now?

Which is your favorite social media site?

Now you can choose any of the above listed to research and see if you want to invest in your savings and watch your money grow.

There are some risks with certain investments. Therefore, be sure to have an adult and financial advisor assist you before you make any decision.

BONUS TIP - CREDIT HISTORY

It is NEVER too early to learn about credit and its importance. The earlier you're aware of what is, the better off you will be.

Credit History is when your spending habits are monitored to judge whether or not you are eligible to receive loans and credit cards. The privilege of credit allows you to purchase things without using physical cash at that particular moment.

Why is your credit history important? Because your entire life revolves around your credit history. If you do not manage your money well starting at the age of 18, you will not be able to purchase a home, a car and sometimes not able to get the job you want.

Credit Score Chart	
Score	Grading
720 and Above	Excellent
680 to 719	Good
620 to 679	Average
580 to 619	Poor
500 to 579	Bad
Less than 500	Miserable

Once you begin working and establishing credit you want to always know where you stand on this list.

3 Important Tips to Remember...If you

1) Pay your bills on time

2) Do not use credit cards unless you have the cash to pay for what you just brought.

3) **NEVER EVER** let anyone use your social security number for their credit. If they can't get approved, chances are they've already ruined their credit.

If you follow these three tips, when you begin earning an income, your credit will stay in the green and your opportunities for home ownership, purchasing a car, starting a business and more will be available to you.

"Life's most persistent and urgent question is: What are you doing for others?"

-Dr. Martin Luther King Jr.

Chapter 6
Serve and Win

Dear Student,

I am writing this letter to encourage you in your quest to develop into aspiring young leaders of the future. Congratulations to you on reaching an important milestone and becoming an actively engaged middle school students and leaders. Sometimes you as young, inexperienced individuals will feel that the world is big an unconquerable which can be overwhelming. The world sometimes labels young people as rebellious and irresponsible. Please don't allow this to distract you. As you continue to evolve into young men and women, the opportunities and choices will be limitless. For the next 5-10 years, you will be making decisions that will not only affect your life but will also affect the lives of many other people.

Currently, I am in the field of academic education at a local Christian College – Nyack College in Rockland, New York in this capacity I have had the opportunity to work with students from various backgrounds, cultures, and life experiences. This has helped to shape my life and service to enrich the lives of others through education. This has been a source of inspiration to me, and I trust that it will motivate you to stay on the path to service and excellence.

It is important that you take advantage of all opportunities provided for you while you are young for this will help you build a portfolio of experiences that will serve as a platform for future roles and opportunities. It is my greatest desire that you will develop a personal testimony about your past, present and future experiences. It is also time for you to begin thinking, praying and planning as you continue to prepare for future leadership and service.

My motto that someone shared with me that I would like to leave you with is "*Good, Better, Best, Never let it rest until your Good gets Better and your Better gets Best*".

I feel confident that you will continue to succeed as students. I urge you to think not just of yourselves but others around you.

Regards,

Cynthia Dorsey

Adjunct Professor, Nyack College

There is a saying that goes it is better to give than to receive. In fact, this is a biblical quote that sums up what it means to be of service. In this chapter, I will discuss the importance of being a person of service and how it could help you to build and grow your resume. First, I would like to share my story of how I landed my first job as a teenager and how I ended up growing my career from volunteering and helping someone.

I was only fifteen years old when I started going to visit a friend of mine who worked at what I thought was a regular office building. I used to go to her office every day after school just to say hello. One day, she asked me to help her with some of her work making phone calls, organizing files and stuffing envelopes (fun right)...lol. I did this for about six months. Then...one day, she came to me and said: "there is a summer camp located in the building and that they were looking to hire summer camp counselors, are you interested?" I told her that I had no idea that there was a summer camp in the building and yes I am interested. She was able to get me an interview and long story short, I got the job. I ended up moving up in the company being promoted to other jobs throughout the organization over the next sixteen years.

How was I able to find such a great opportunity at such a young age? I did eight key things that can be duplicated by anyone reading this, especially you if you're looking to build a resume and gain new skills that will make you attractive and marketable in the career world. Today I will share three my top three.

Key One: Be of service. Think about people you know who have jobs and ask if they need help. If you do not know anyone, that's fine. There are plenty of organizations who could use volunteers. To begin, search for organizations on websites where they list various volunteer opportunities and select one that is a great fit for you. See **chapter 7** for a list of websites to find volunteer opportunities.

Key Two: Treat your volunteer opportunity like a paying job. Yes, this opportunity is not something you are going to be paid for. However, in the end, it is a great possibility that the organization could hire you. With this in mind, treat this as if you are a paid employee. Be professional, show up on time and last, be the best volunteer they ever had by over delivering. What does this mean? This could mean showing up earlier, staying late, or asking for additional job duties if you know you can successfully do them within your regular job duties. These things will assure that the organization you are volunteering for will remember you and think of you if and when a paid position becomes available.

Key Three: Be intentional. What I mean by this is that you shouldn't volunteer with an organization with the expectation of them offering you a paid position. When you volunteer, do it because you truly want to, and you are interested in helping the organization. If you are being of service only to get something in return, your actions will show through your work. When you are intentional, you will go above and beyond because it is something you want to do. Others will see this, and you will be compensated. Your payment will come in various ways. Remember, payment can come in many ways such as a letter of recommendation, mentorship, and knowledge. Getting hired would be the icing on the cake.

Serve & Win Activity

Revisit your dream board and look at what you said you want to do in the future. Now jump to chapter 7, and pick one of the websites that connect you to volunteer opportunities, and search for one in your neighborhood that is a good fit for you. For example, if you put on your board that you want to become a veterinarian, you can do a search through the website you selected or you can simply do a Google search using these key words "volunteer opportunities for teens at veterinarian" in (whatever city and state) you reside.

Other examples: Churches, Nonprofit organizations

Choose 3 Company's /Organizations that you want to volunteer with,

Name of company: _____

Address of company: _____

Contact Person Name: _____

Contact Person Phone: _____ Email: _____

Volunteer Position Title: _____

Volunteer Job Description or Responsibilities: _____

_____

_____

_____

Name of company: _____

Address of company: _____

Contact Person Name: _____

Contact Person Phone: _____ Email: _____

Volunteer Position Title: _____

Volunteer Job Description or Responsibilities: _____

_____

_____

_____

Name of company: _____

Address of company: _____

Contact Person Name: _____

Contact Person Phone: _____ Email: _____

Volunteer Position Title: _____

Volunteer Job Description or Responsibilities: _____

_____

_____

"When you believe in your dream and your vision, then it begins to attract its own resources. No one was born to be a failure."

-Myles Munroe

Chapter 7
Resources

NIA CAMPBELL
High School
123 ABC LANE
Cell: 555-555-7777
Email: NiaCampbell@abc.com

SUMMARY
High school student with 7 years of being on honor roll, experienced in child care, event planning providing the best customer service experience for all of my clients. I am dependable, punctual and committed. Most of all I am trustworthy and responsible.

EXPERIENCE
Baby Sitter – Brooklyn, NY   *2012*
Summary of responsibilities: Cared for two young children, ages five and six. Transported both children home after school and engaged them in educational and recreational activities including trips to the park, educational videos, and homework. Lastly, I also prepared small meals including snack.

Event Planner – Brooklyn, NY   *2012*
Summary of responsibilities: Organized, a summertime family gathering for 100 guests in honor of the passing of a family member.   Sent invitations electronically and via telephone, created a Facebook page for the event to track guests who rsvp'd. Assisted with food preparation, entertainment and set up.

ACTIVITIES
Justice Panel Member at High School   *2012 - 2014*
Summary of responsibilities: Provide conflict resolution groups with at-risk students at Lyons Community High School with a goal of decreasing suspensions and expulsions.

AWARDS
Honor Roll at High School for 7 Quarters

AFFILIATIONS
Girl Scout – Brooklyn, NY   *2012 - Present*
Girl Scouts of America

References furnished upon request

96

Jeremiah Hewitt
123 Alphabet Lane
New York, NY 10000
Mobile: 111-222-3333
Email: jhewitt@gmail.com

June 5, 2016

Madelyn Wright
Administrative Assistant
Automotive Center
1 Frontier Avenue
New York, NY 10000

Dear Ms. Wright

Re: Part-time Shop Assistant, Automotive Center

It was great speaking with you on the phone this morning. As discussed, I am writing to submit my resume for part-time shop assistant at the Automotive Center. I'm currently a 9th grade student attending Urban Assembly for Engineering and Technology. I would be available to work shifts all weekend and after 2:30 pm on Tuesdays and Wednesdays.

My dad used to bring his car for repairs before we moved out of the area. I enjoyed watching the mechanic work on the cars in the yard. In addition, the staff would always answer my questions about what they were working on. I believe my friendly and approachable personality and my resilient work ethic would make me a treasured addition to the company.

I communicate well with others, and I am able to adapt to various types of workplace changes with great ease. I'm also a team player, as demonstrated by my achievements in the school basketball team.

I have attached my resume and am available to attend an interview at your earliest convenience.

I look forward to the opportunity to discuss how I can contribute to your team.

Yours sincerely
[Sign here]
Jeremiah Hewitt

Sample thank you letter

Jeremiah Hewitt
123 Alphabet Lane
New York, NY 11111
Mobile: 111-222-3333
Email: jhewitt@gmail.com

Charlene R. Nathaniel
Human Resource Manager
Dare 2 Dream Leaders Inc.
123 ABC Drive
Brooklyn, NY 11210

Dear Ms. Nathaniel:

Thank you for giving me the opportunity to interview with Dare 2 Dream Leaders Inc. for the position of volunteer coordinator on August 1st. I really enjoyed meeting you and spending the morning learning more about your organization and the position that is available.

I feel that my experience and education have prepared me to work for Dare 2 Dream Leaders Inc., and I look forward to being able to learn more about engaging volunteers for your company.

Again, thank you for your time. I am looking forward to hearing from you soon.

Sincerely,

Jeremiah Hewitt

Examples of how to dress for success

"You cannot climb the ladder of success dressed in the costume of failure."

- Zig Ziglar

Sample Allowance Contract between Parent and Child

I, Karizma am seeking to enter into a contract for my allowance terms with my parent Regina Walker for weekly payment. I am asking for $ 20 to be paid every Saturday by 12 :00 pm. Below is a list of jobs that that we can use to create a weekly job chart.

Week of : _____	M	Tu	W	Th	F	S
Directions: Pick 5 chores to be completed each week by checking off the chore below. Place an X next to the day the chore should be completed. **Each additional chore over 5 will generate an extra $1.** See example below.						Pay Day
☐ Clear your business voice mails	X					
☐ Check your emails						
☐ Proof read your letters						
☐ Do your laundry		X				
☐ Organize your closet						
☐ Clean the inside of your car			x			
☐ Wash the window in the house						
☐ Clean the bathroom sink, toilet, mirror				x		
☐ Organize kitchen cabinets						
☐ Clean pet cages					x	
☐ Feed pets					x	
☐ Take out garbage						

I, _____ agree to this contract. Date: _____

Parent Signature: _____

Youth Signature: _____

Allowance Contract between parent and child

I, _____am seeking to enter into a contract for my allowance terms with my parent _____for weekly payment. I am asking for $_____ to be paid every Saturday by _____:_____ am or pm. Below is a list of jobs that that we can use to create a weekly job chart.

I,

Week of : _____							
Directions: Pick 5 chores to be completed each week by checking off the chore below. Place an X next to the day the chore should be completed. **Each additional chore over 5 will generate an extra $1.** See example below.	M	Tu	W	Th	F	S Pay Day
☐ Clear your business voice mails						
☐ Check your emails						
☐ Proof read your letters						
☐ Do your laundry						
☐ Organize your closet						
☐ Clean the inside of your car						
☐ Wash the window in the house						
☐ Clean the bathroom sink, toilet, mirror						
☐ Organize kitchen cabinets						
☐ Clean pet cages						
☐ Feed pets						
☐ Take out garbage						

_____ agree to this contract. Date: _____

Parent Signature: _____

Youth Signature: _____

Dream board aka Vision board creation - Create online, save and print

- http://happyblackwoman.com/how-to-make-a-digital-vision-board/
- http://fototalisman.com/

Resume & Cover Letters | Interviewing | Job Search

- https://www.careerkids.com/MyFirstResume.aspx
- http://www.myfuture.com/careers/
- http://www.boostapal.com/find-teen-jobs
- http://www.gcflearnfree.org/jobsearch

Entrepreneurship | Business Plan | Innovation

- https://www.ted.com/playlists/129/ted_under_20
- http://www.teenbusiness.com/
- https://www.sba.gov/content/young-entrepreneurs-series

Teen Financial Empowerment –Saving| Budgeting| Credit| Investing

- http://www.themint.org/

Community Service

- http://www.ysop.org/
- http://www.nycservice.org/
- https://www.newyorkcares.org/youth-volunteering
- https://www.dosomething.org/us
- http://www.lionsheartservice.org/
- http://www.dare2dreamleaders.org

"You can only become truly accomplished at something you love. Don't make money your goal. Instead, pursue the things you love doing and then do them so well that people can't take their eyes off of you."

-Maya Angelou

Chapter 8
Affirmations & Journal

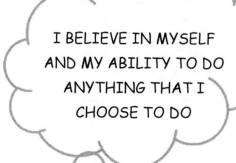

I BELIEVE IN MYSELF
AND MY ABILITY TO DO
ANYTHING THAT I
CHOOSE TO DO

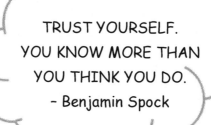

TRUST YOURSELF.
YOU KNOW MORE THAN
YOU THINK YOU DO.
– Benjamin Spock

Dream Big
Set Goals
Take Action!

I AM
SUCCESSFUL IN
WHATEVER I DO.

_____

_____

_____

_____

_____

_____

_____

_____

_____

_____

_____

_____

_____

_____

_____

_____

I AM A GOOD PERSON
AND
I AM PROUD TO BE ME

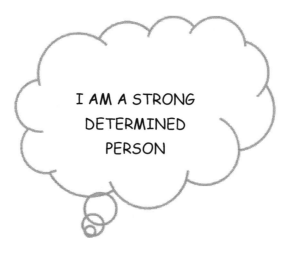

I AM A STRONG
DETERMINED
PERSON

I BELIEVE IN
MYSELF AND MY
ABILITIES.

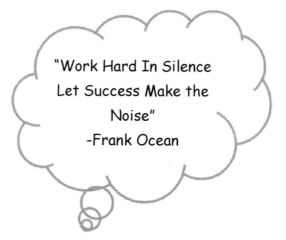

"Work Hard In Silence
Let Success Make the
Noise"
-Frank Ocean

_____
_____
_____
_____
_____
_____
_____
_____
_____
_____
_____
_____
_____
_____
_____

I enjoy challenges.
I take them head on and
win over them.
I am always successful.
Success is in my blood.
I am always successful.
Success is in my blood.

"I CAN BECAUSE I THINK I CAN.

I AM BECASUE I THINK I AM.

I WILL BECAUSE I WANT TO.

I AM THE HERO OF MY OWN STORY.

I WILL ACHIEVE ANYTHING I WANT TO ACHIEVE.

I AM LIMITLESS; I KNOW NO BOUNDARIES.

I WILL SUCCEED.

I AM SUCCESS.

I AM FREE.

I AM GREAT TODAY."

"The future belongs to those who believe in the beauty of their dreams."

-Eleanor Roosevelt

Conclusion

Congratulations! You have just completed Beyond Career day, your guide to success. Now that you are done, what will you do with all of this information? Use it every day I hope! Let's recap some of things you should have learned after finishing Beyond Career Day. You should now be able to create your very own dream board packed with your smart goals, dreams, and aspirations. Take time to look at your dream board every day as a reminder of your goals and once per month to see what you've accomplished. It will amaze you. Remember dreams plus action equals success!

It is my hope that after reading and completing the activities in this book, you have learned more about yourself as a person and you should have a vision of what you want to accomplish in the near future. In chapter 3, you were provided with career etiquette tips that will help you create your resume and how to prepare for a job interview/volunteer opportunity to ensure that you have a winning interview. Once you get your first job, you should be able to apply what you have learned in chapter 5 which includes how to budget, which will keep you from spending all of your money at the mall or on food after school. You also learned about the importance of saving and investing and why having good credit is important for your future plans such as when purchasing a home or car. Trust me you don't want to hurt your credit. Remember you heard it first here!

Last, remember that you have unique skills and talents within you that could be used to start a business. Having a job where you work for someone else does not have to be your only source of income but use your unique skills and talents to start your own business as discussed in chapter 4. Use the quotes and affirmations in chapter 8 to keep you motivated by choosing one per day or week to say out loud at the start of your day. Beyond Career Day was written to equip you with tools to help you succeed beyond school and beyond your career. You can succeed in every aspect of your life, just believe in yourself, do the work and know that I believe in you!

About the Author

Ijana Nathaniel is the mother of two amazing children, Jeremiah (13), the future basketball star and Nia (3), the smart and sassy little lady. They both keep her busy with basketball games, community recreation, and other activities. Ijana has a passion and truly loves working with youth in networking and creating opportunities to help them follow their dreams and passion.

In 2010, Ms. Nathaniel became the Founder and President of Dare 2 Dream Leaders Inc., a 501c3 nonprofit youth organization based in Brooklyn, NY serving Middle School and High School students. The organization provides mentoring and educational programs to help today's youth gain financial, career entrepreneurial skills. Dare 2 Dream hosts an annual youth summit free to over 100 Middle & High School students throughout New York City exposing them to our sponsors, professionals, connecting them to resources, network opportunities with their peers and allowing them to have fun with our invited entertainment.

In 2016, Ijana became a self-published author with her first book Dare 2 Dream Leaders Inc., Present Beyond Career Day: A Success Guide for Middle School Youth.

Ms. Nathaniel holds a Master's Degree in Organizational Leadership from Nyack College, with specialties in curriculum design, workshop implementation, and panel discussion, mentoring and public speaking.

Want to extend the invitation to Ijana Nathaniel to share her story, insight and expertise on youth empowerment with your audience? Send invitation inquiries to ijananathaniel@gmail.com

Bulk Ordering Information: Special discounts are available for quantity purchases by schools, associations, corporations and others. For details, see order form or contact the offices of Ijana Nathaniel using the above or below information.

https://about.me/ijana.nathaniel

ijananathaniel@gmail.com

347-560-9836

Social Media Platforms

@ijananathaniel

Order Form

Customer Information   (Please Print Clearly)

(Name: First, Middle Initial, Last)	(E-mail)

(Street Address)

(City)	(State)	(Zip Code)

PAYMENT INFORMATION (Choose One):

☐ MC ☐ Visa   Billing Address (Street, City, State & Zip)

(Credit Card Number)	(Exp. Date)	CVC

☐ Cash

Quantity	Price	Total

Thank You for Your Order

*Bulk Order pricing available, please call 347-560-9836

Made in the USA
Middletown, DE
24 September 2016